This
Naure Storybook
belongs to:

_____

_____

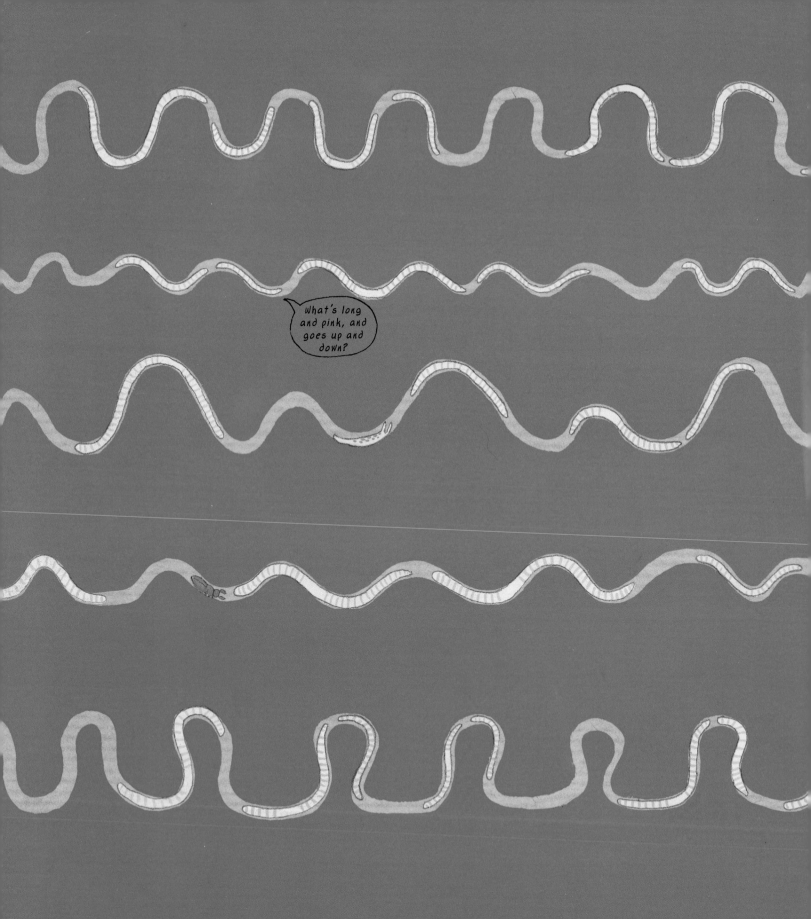

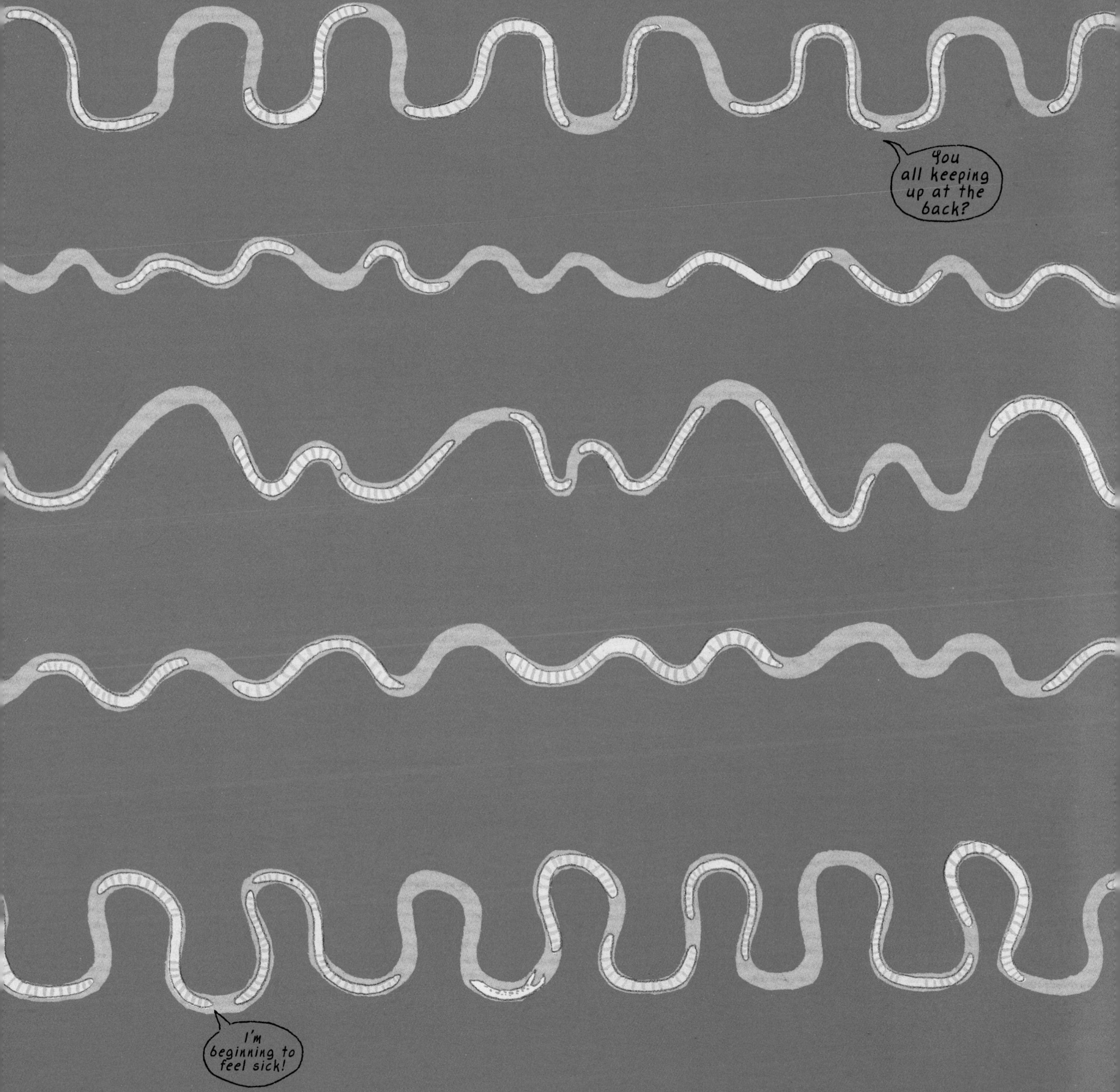
You all keeping up at the back?
I'm beginning to feel sick!

First published 2009 by Walker Books Ltd
87 Vauxhall Walk, London SE11 5HJ

This edition published 2015

1 2 3 4 5 6 7 8 9 10

This book has been typeset in
Marker Finepoint and Providence

Printed in China

British Library Cataloguing in Publication Data:
a catalogue record for this book is available
from the British Library

ISBN 978-1-4063-6704-1

www.walker.co.uk

For Jack
V. F.

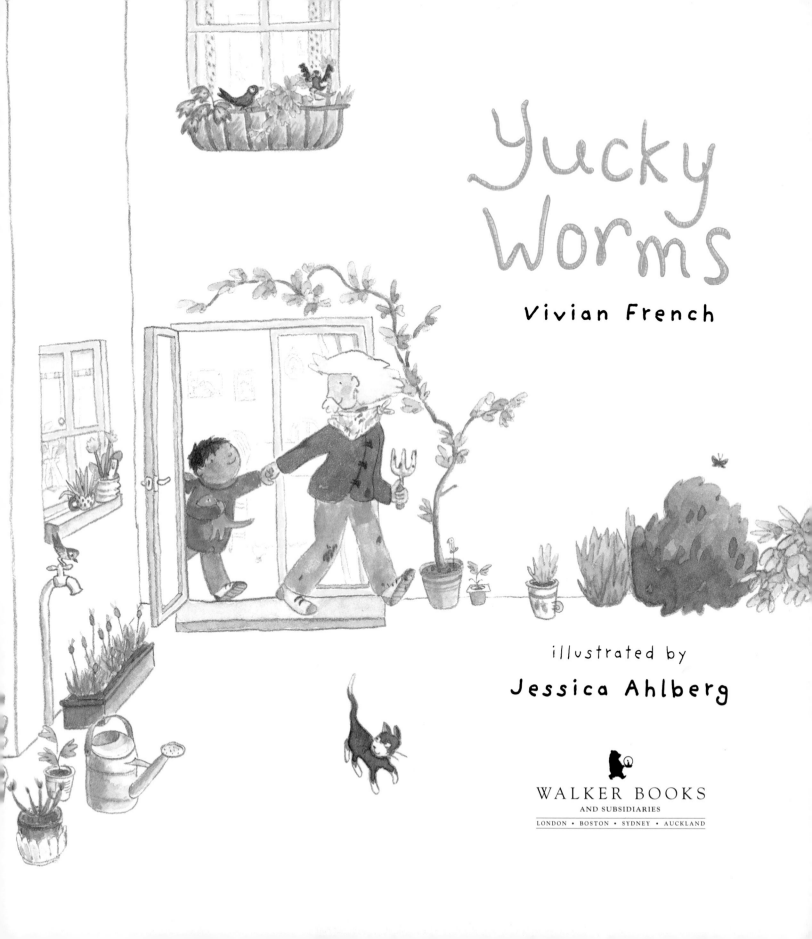

Yucky Worms

Vivian French

illustrated by

Jessica Ahlberg

WALKER BOOKS
AND SUBSIDIARIES
LONDON · BOSTON · SYDNEY · AUCKLAND

One day when I was
in Gran's garden,
Gran dug up a slimy
slithery
wiggly
worm.

"Yuck!" I said. "Throw it away!"

"Throw it away?" Gran looked horrified.

"Would you throw away one of your friends?"

"You can't be friends with a worm," I said.

"You can't even tell which end is which."

"Yes you can! Watch."
Gran put the worm down.

It gave a kind of
squirmy wriggle
and disappeared
really fast,
pointy end first.

As the rounded end vanished,
Gran said, "There goes its tail."
I bent down to look, and I could see
it had left a little tunnel.

In most gardens
there will be about
20 worms in every
square metre of earth.

"Where's it gone?" I asked.
"Home," Gran said.
"It's an earthworm.
It lives in the earth."

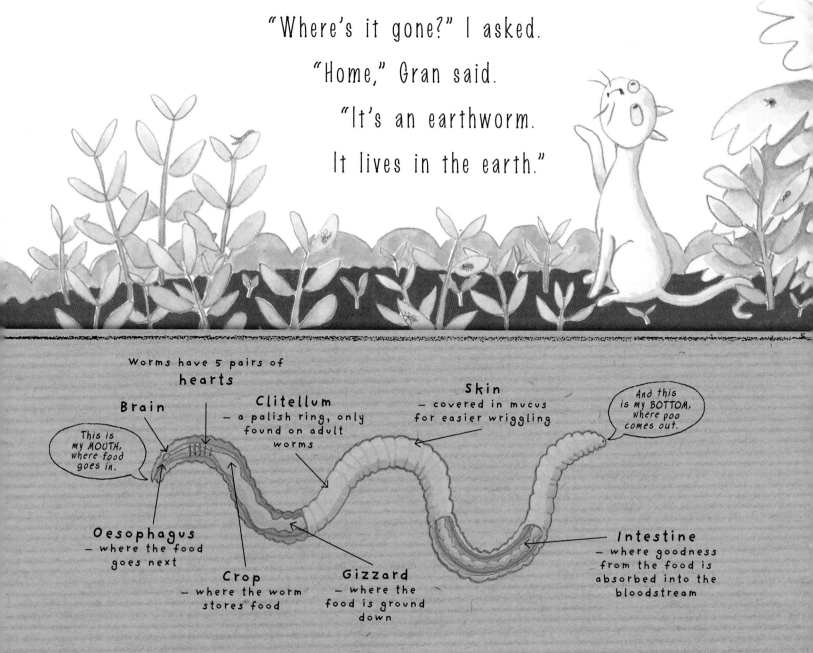

Worms have 5 pairs of
hearts

Brain

Clitellum
– a palish ring, only
found on adult
worms

Skin
– covered in mucus
for easier wriggling

*This is
MY MOUTH,
where food
goes in.*

*And this
is MY BOTTOM,
where poo
comes out.*

Oesophagus
– where the food
goes next

Crop
– where the worm
stores food

Gizzard
– where the
food is ground
down

Intestine
– where goodness
from the food is
absorbed into the
bloodstream

"Does it eat earth too?"
I wanted to know.
"It eats tiny tiny stones and bits of grit,"
Gran told me, "but worms eat other things
as well, like rotting leaves
and flowers and fruit and dead insects.
They specially like eating at night,
when it's cool.

10

Worms come
above ground to
find things
to eat too...

Nice
and rotten.
Just how I
like it.

They pull
their food
back down
as they wriggle
into the
earth again.

The stones and grit help to grind
everything up in the worm's stomach,
and then the worm
poos it back out."

Zzzzz.

11

Gran pointed
at the flowerbed.
"LOOK! Can you see?"
I bent down — and I saw a
weird long curly worm made of earth.
"That's worm poo," Gran said. "It's called a cast.
You know when you recycle things? Well, worms
do it too. There's still a lot of goodness
left in the things a worm eats, and when the
goodness comes out again as poo, it helps
plants to grow BIG and STRONG.
And as the worms move about, under and over the earth,
the poo gets spread around the garden...

That's why
worms are my friends."
Gran gave me a thumbs-up.
"It's not just their poo
that's good for plants.
The tunnels they dig
loosen the soil — so
roots can stretch out and
air and rain water
can get in."

Worms' poo is so fine and crumbly it never blocks their tunnels.

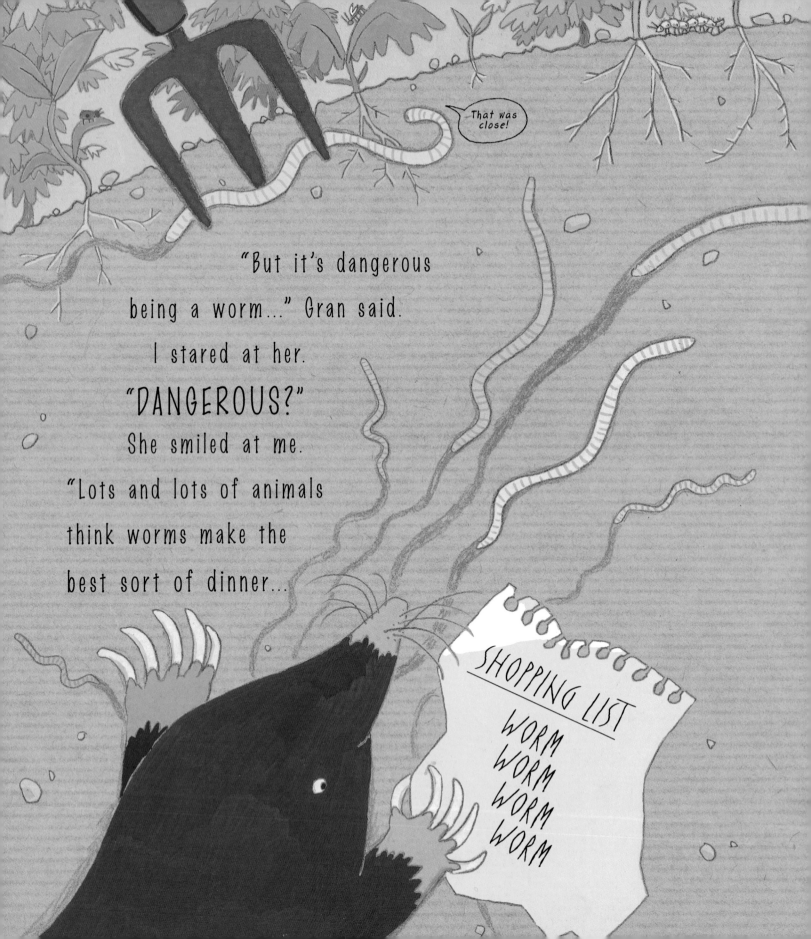

"That was close!"

"But it's dangerous being a worm..." Gran said.

I stared at her.

"DANGEROUS?"

She smiled at me.

"Lots and lots of animals think worms make the best sort of dinner...

SHOPPING LIST

WORM
WORM
WORM
WORM

Birds **LOVE** them — and

so do moles, badgers, frogs,

hedgehogs and foxes — even some slugs eat worms.

And human beings slice them with spades

and spike them with forks — it's a tough life."

"Cutting them in half doesn't hurt them, Gran," I said.

"They just turn into two worms, and keep on growing."

Gran shook her head. "Poor worms.

Lots of people think that, but it's not true."

She put her fork down.

"Time for a snack!"

A worm's tail can regrow if it's cut off, but cutting a worm in half will kill it.

17

Gran had tea, and I had orange juice.
"Can I dig a worm up?" I asked.
"If it rains," Gran said, "the worms
will come up on their own."

Worms breathe through their skins.
They don't mind the earth around them
being wet, but if their tunnels are flooded,
they come up to the surface to breathe.

I took a biscuit. "What if it doesn't rain?"
Gran winked at me. "We'll use
the watering can, and pretend."
I finished my biscuit as fast as I could.
"Can we trick the worms NOW?"

Gran went to fill the
watering can
and I watered
the earth.
Then I stood back —
I didn't want worms
chewing at my shoes.

"They only put their heads out," Gran promised. "And it'll be a while before they do."

21

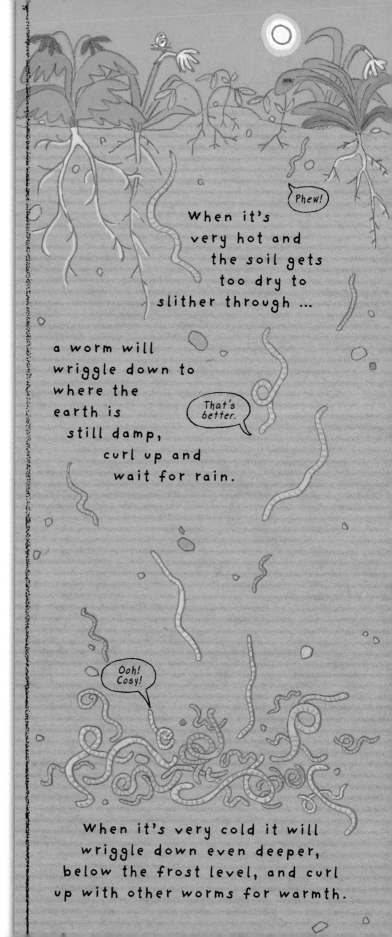

Phew!

When it's very hot and the soil gets too dry to slither through ...

a worm will wriggle down to where the earth is still damp, curl up and wait for rain.

That's better.

Ooh! Cosy!

When it's very cold it will wriggle down even deeper, below the frost level, and curl up with other worms for warmth.

Gran was right. I had time to eat
two more biscuits before she said,
"Look!"

"WOW," I said.
I could just see the tip of
a worm above the earth.
"Now watch this..."
Gran stamped, and the
worm disappeared.

"Did it see you?" I asked.
Gran shook her head.
"Worms don't have eyes.
They feel vibrations,
though—and a thump
like that might mean
Hungry Bird landing.
DANGER!"

Gran dug her fork in the ground. Up came lots of earth and wriggly worms. She picked one up, and washed it in the watering can.

"Mustn't drop it," she said. "They can't swim."

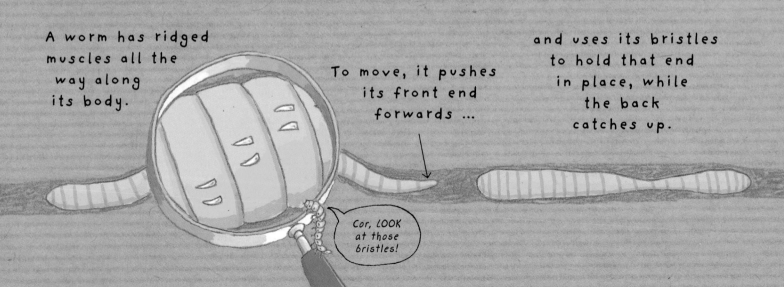

A worm has ridged muscles all the way along its body.

To move, it pushes its front end forwards ...

and uses its bristles to hold that end in place, while the back catches up.

Cor, LOOK at those bristles!

Gran put the clean worm on some paper and held it near my ear. I could hear a tiny rustling noise.
"What's that?"
"They're covered in little bristles," Gran said.
"The bristles and their muscles help them move."

The back end bristles stop the worm from sliding backwards,

while the front end tunnels forwards again into the earth

Cheerio!

... just like a slinky toy.

"I've got muscles too!"
I bent my arm so Gran could see.

"If you've got so many muscles," she said,
"maybe you'd like to help me plant my
sunflower seedlings?"
"OK," I nodded, and then I thought
of something.

"When I go to school on
Monday I'm going to say that I've got lots of new friends!"
"Good idea," Gran said.
"Actually," I said, "I might not actually
say they're worms..."

27

HOW TO BE A WORMOLOGIST!

LOOK OUT FOR...

* Worm casts in your garden, or in the park.
* Leaves sticking up out of the earth.
* Worms on the surface after rain.

EXPERIMENT BY...

* Watering a dry patch of grass or earth and watching to see if worms come up.
* Tapping on the ground to see if you can make a worm believe it's raining.
* Carefully digging up a forkful of earth and counting how many worms you find.

28

A WORM IN THE HAND...

When you pick up a worm, remember to be respectful; a worm is a living creature.

* Check how it feels. Is it smooth? Is it slimy?
Can you feel the bristles?
* Watch how it moves.
* Is it a youngster or an adult? (Adults have a clitellum — a yellow ring around their body.)
* Put the worm back on newly-dug earth,
and watch how it wriggles away.

Always wash your hands after touching worms.

Index

Look up the pages
to find out about
all these wormy things.
Don't forget to
look at both kinds
of word —
this kind
and
this kind.

*

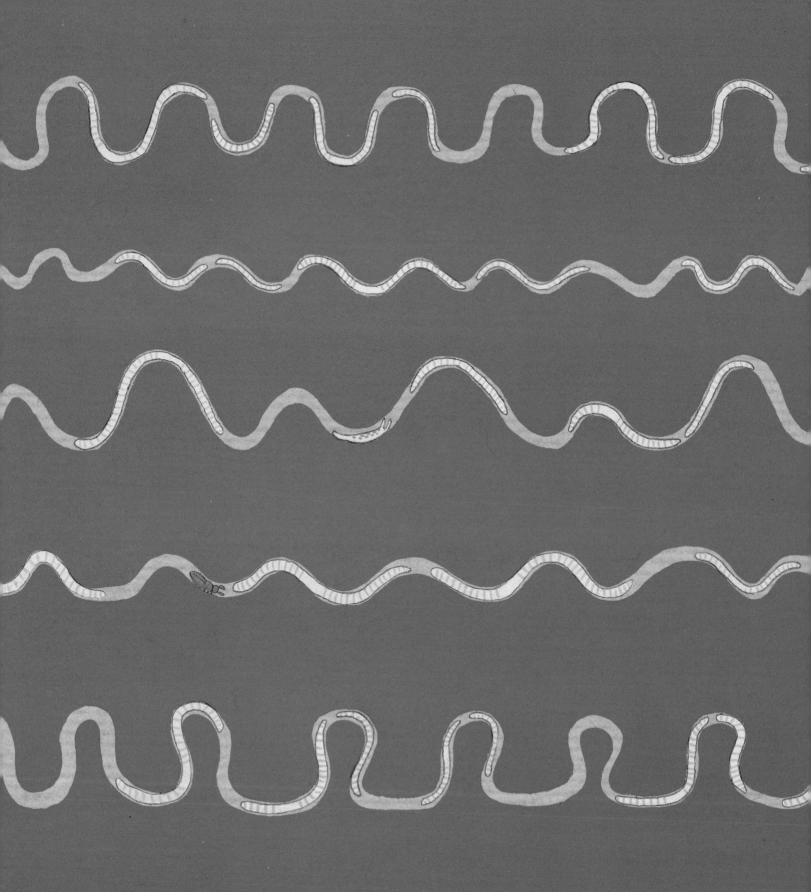